CENTURY

DEAD

CENTER

&

OTHER

POEMS

CENTURY DEAD CENTER & OTHER POEMS

George Economou

Left Hand Books

Copyright © 1997 by George Economou. All rights reserved.

The publisher wishes to thank the John W. and Clara C. Higgins Foundation for financial assistance granted as well as the Pauline Oliveros Foundation for their continued general support.

Left Hand Books website: http://www.lefthandbooks.com/lhb

Cover: *(not with sunsray)* by George Economou. Water color and pastel on paper. 5" x 7."
Frontispiece: *Piers* by George Economou. Ink on paper. 12" x 18."

Designed by Bryan McHugh.

ISBN 1-880516-23-3

Manufactured in the United States of America.

Some of these poems appeared previously in the following publications: *Aggregate Images, American Poetry Review, Another Chicago Magazine, Ashen Meal, Backwoods Broadsides Chaplets, Correspondence, Cover, First Intensity, Forkroads, Grand Street, Harvard Review, Mandorla, Niagra, Nimrod, Poems for the Millenium, Poetry New York, Sulfur,* and *Texture. Voluntaries* was first published by the Corycian Press. "An Evening in Kingfisher" was previously published in *harmonies & fits,* Point Riders Press.

I would like to thank the Rockefeller Foundation for a residency during the spring of 1993 at its Bellagio Study and Conference Center on Lake Como, Italy, where the "Bell-Haiku" were written and the title poem of this collection was begun.

This book is for Rochelle.

CONTENTS

VE/VJ — 3
May 7, 1995 — 4
(not with sunsray) — 6

CENTURY DEAD CENTER — 9

4 PAINTINGS — 41
Mother and Child — 41
Ommatidium — 42
L'âge d'or — 43
1892 — 44

1892 — 45

VOLUNTARIES — 55

PLAY/FABLES — 79

NASHVILLANELLE AND OTHER RIMES — 83
Nashvillanelle — 84
Love's Letter ψ — 85
Kyrielle (A Song for September) — 86
Lament of the Mafioso Maker — 87
Il Gran Veglio di Creta — 89

TRANSLATIONS 91

Hedylos from the Greek Anthology, # 199 92
The Girl Next Door 93
from C.P. Cavafy 94
    Half an Hour 94
    In the Month of Athyr 95
    The City 96
    According to the Recipes of Ancient Greco- 97
       Syrian Magicians
from George Seferis 98
    Les Anges Sont Blancs 98
    The Cats of St. Nicholas 101
from José Pascual Buxó 104
    Etruscan Museum 104

REMEMBERING AN UNSHARED NARRATIVE 109

X-RAY FINISH 113

List of Titles for Stories Never to be Written 114
    in the Short Story Writer's Notebook
In the Winner's Circle 118
An Evening in Kingfisher 119
Bell-Haiku 122

CENTURY DEAD CENTER & OTHER POEMS

VE/VJ

Name: Hans Rudelsheim
Date of Birth: 1922
Place of Birth: Kampen, Netherlands

MAY 7, 1995

Is it half our century
already since it opened
the black hole at its center?
Televised now round the world
it still holds our worst surprise
(a click away, rescue dogs
work the vertical wound in
downtown Oklahoma City).
After the garnish of queen
Mother's message of courage
and solo Spitfire's skycross
tribute to Winston Churchill,
it comes down to this story,
printed on a folded five
by seven card and retold
to a condition of in-
eradicability:
        Dogless,
the Gestapo agent failed
to sniff out Hans Rudelsheim,
hidden behind some clothes in
his friend Ina's bathroom closet.
"And this is the closet…,"
she said casually as she could
and the search of her house ended.
A brief satisfaction, till
later that year, '43
March, when the mouth of a neighbor's

friend opened against him and
swallowed him whole *(Hold not thy
peace, O God of my praise)*
as easy as counting to four:
alive in Leiden—eins, zwei,
drei, vier—in Treblinka smoke.
It smelled for miles but they
denied it, though not godless.

Hans was born to a Jewish family in the small Dutch town of Kampen. His father worked as a tailor, and he taught Hans about the tailoring trade.

1933-39: Hans was a skilled tailor, and an accomplished pianist as well. Inquisitive about all subjects, Hans loved to read and to keep abreast of current events.

1940-43: When the Jews in the Dutch provinces were ordered to relocate to Amsterdam in January 1942, the Rudelsheims complied. In early 1943, while in hiding with a Christian family near Leiden, Hans sneaked out to visit his friend Ina. Suddenly, a German came to Ina's door. Hans hid behind some clothes in a bathroom closet. The German searched the house and when they reached the bathroom, Ina opened the dark closet, saying as casually as she could, "... and this is the closet." Satisfied no one else was in the house, the German left.

In March 1943 Hans was betrayed. He was deported, and perished in a concentration camp.

Story and photo from the collection of The United States Holocaust Museum. Card No. 1234

(not with sunsray)

Sine aer
        nosethirles singed
                (not with sunsray)
                            a seared wound
of windows closed
        upon a mortal distant
                sing-song guttural
                        unbreathed.

        Wave upon wave jammed
        at the shore as if a door
        had closed behind them.
        A sea of faces fluttered
        in a melt of tide and time
        that will wait and waits
        for each and every one.
        The waters vex the wind
        and all things earthen fire.

Runs lid into
      iris as jade
            liquified
                  into river
                          charnelled
                                with mothers

and lovers
  under the urine
    reddened sky
      fulsome with
        liberated X ray.

    That life's no more than cover
    from a shower sun flares never
    warned will be no more no more.
    This handiwork unveils birds
    and nouns obliterated—no cover
    from or for the monument
    of victory in August:
              our charred meditation.

CENTURY DEAD CENTER

1

When it happened it didn't happen in newsreel. Its history happened to. Easier to take home in black and white and head off the passing moment through the air, so sharp and short. He dies from a burst to the chest in a second, hangs from the boots forever. When it happened it was real news. Then turned black and white. Death's proof develops in black and white till it comes as news for you, real and stark and possessing the air it passes through on its way to the black and white house where it rewinds and waits.

2

There wasn't any blood. Still it was read and flowed for generations. Of poison. For centuries of poison. The immunity was colossal. Its epidermal imprint: tracing veins monumental and saturated. Whose inner walls never showed. Not until their bursting point. Then there was blood. Assayed, drop by drop, for centuries. Generations. The poisonous immunity. Painted with used bandages. Wrap and tie, wrap and tie. Educed, the poison knot. For generations. For centuries. To the bursting point. Time for some blood again.

3

The archaeologist begins talking. Her elbows and ribs ache. Nothing she says lines up with her knee-prints. Nothing she feels can fill their bowls in the sand. She stands up, they disappear, fatten the air. There are things about her life she cannot retrieve. Remember as needing it, even. Right now she can think only about hot tea and ice water. Wanting to fill herself with them. And to talk a little longer. Again, she kneels and bends over her prey. Stops talking. No one sees her put in the final touches. Which takes hours. All out.

4

You should be able to get there by foot. Besides there's no other way. No other choice. For you. Even if you had a map, there would be surprises. Bad to worse. So prepare. Point yourselves in this black direction. Let us keep it nameless. Like your destination. For now. So if you don't get there, you've still gotten there. In a manner, bad to worse, of speaking. A map? We will make one up for you. Name of your destination? Let us put it this way. If you get there from here, it's another way of getting from bad to worse. We guarantee it.

5

And the wife tied herself to her dying husband and they fell into the water—from the villa chamber overhanging the lake. A legend tells a lady pushed her lover and he fell into the lake from a point high above the water. Storied faithless lovers trip, the true leap. The poet strips her fingers of her rings and wears her mother's fur. True to the fear overhanging her perforated days, she rises to a point high above her balance and falls into the lake of fumes and fading music. Torn from life's book, she trips into story.

6

The mythomaniac's talking his guts out. His waving hands move back horizons. The others step lively to keep up with him. Sky. His anecdotes secure with them, down to earth with them. Tumbling, then fettered to eye and ear. Slowed up to meet their measure. They cannot stand to talk to him. They cannot stand not to listen to him. They tread water he walks on. Cannot keep up with him. They cannot help but slow him down. A rope and a rock, or a noose and a knife. Still they will listen, rapt, to the last sounds he shoots.

7

The unspeakable. May be screamed. Sung into remembrance. Who most listen for it to the capture are speechless in its honor. Then spill. Submit to its surrendering in them. White flags of terror turned to dreams of lost and found. So the-couldn't-be-worse is finally something to write home about. Put it this way. What good is all the evil we've done if we do not speak of it? The unspeakable. May be screamed. Worn like a badge. A tattooed number. A poem. Let the record show: on Justitia's tab. Then hold your peace or jump.

8

The prophet wants a good feed. Even if he has to fast for it, as long as it comes sooner or later as ordered. Proof well-worth the wait. It's in the eating. Order that justifies this mess of explanations and excuses: this steady diet of phenomenals. So the prophet waits and works in the dark room of his desire where he alone sees his proofs coagulate. He picks at them lightly, his taste buds awakening to their salty continuity. Then mouths the full picture and swallows it whole, even if it curdles the blood, it's a feast of cogency. Wait.

9

At first the cries were music to their ears. The march of life. Step. Fuck. Step. Stop to have a portrait taken: Proud Papa in Brown Shirt holding the Infant Christa. A composition worth careful study. And the music, the music was colossal. Filled the air from sea to lung. And the terrified new cries were lost in its volume. Work. Much work to be done. To the music. To the march. To found the center of the century. Black hole on earth. End of the line and final pitch where the wailing infant flies from his hand into an open grave.

10

There is always a chance that in some corner five or six will join hands in a dance to their happy, good hour. You can be sure they'll eventually twirl out of the picture, though the black iconography of their chance always lingers there. Traces of the saving vision they will kill each other for. To have been holding hands in that circle, to have filled one of those spaces of touching choreography, is their dream. To launder death. After all they have done and made of their matters. There is always a chance. In some corner. To slip white.

11

Justitia keeps a column in her account book under the heading **Miscarriages**. Those against the public she writes in red. Against the person in black. Giving the illusion there may be an actual counterpoise between them. Or that the red may one day be repaid, the black deducted from liabilities assumed at birth. The word **Audit** drives her to knock back another boilermaker. But she keeps on doing her job, steady in her seat. Just now she assures a woman greater miscarriage may lie in full term allowed.

12

And the prophet had a dream that the world's fundamentalists convened in the palm of his hand. One from each of the world's great religions. And they began to dig what they called their "deep places" in the skin of his hand and to sing what they called their "joyful noise." They came to understand each other and to see they shared enemies and made righteous arrangements to deal them bloody amens. And the prophet in his dream took a deep breath and tried to blow them off his hand: Awoke suddenly with fists clenched.

13

The tomb's inventory was inconclusive. Especially the petrified figure of the tattooed hermaphrodite. Slightly yet definitely larger than life. Naked yet utterly clothed in its epidermal design, whose imprint seemed to saturate rather than merely to cover its form with its stone-tight wordless pattern. The archaeologist wondered if it had been part of a sarcophagus, but it stood free amidst the fragments of living with no trace or whiff of human remains. What a find! Then inside each of its thighs she made out `refugee` and `colonialist`.

14

By the time they put him away, he was saying things like the best man he ever knew was a cat. And to fancy that with a host of cats at his back he, the Doctor of Immunologics, waging phagocytotic war, could hold the world's evil in check. You eat what you are, he said. But they laughed and named him Dr. Phagopsychotic and put him further away, in a cell that consumed him. Then he stopped saying and only thought things. That they had it so wrong, yet they'd come and see he'd swum away and fathom his true kind, a manner of fish.

15

You and I, we are each the man for the job. The Peter and the Paul, so to speak, of this operation. I build the camps well enough to do the deed, poorly enough to destroy any proof it was ever done. *Alles verschwinden, mon ami.* Even the paper for documents. Which brings us to your department, keeper of the flame of letters. Your very own vanishing act, an impassivity of release: to be at a loss, not for your dear words, but of knowing what they may be up to. Never face to face, always through a glass darkly, in allegories of elsewhere.

16

But then shall I know even as also I am known. That's when you're dead, right? And think you're saved, a perfect transparency? But in my life, I didn't know myself till Jesus hopped onto my right shoulder when I was fourteen, walking barefoot down a red dirt road. "I will be your good ol' boy all your life," he said in my ear, "and will walk, like a mama, by your side long as you listen to me." I tell you this lightening happened here, and there'll be plenty of dying for lack of that birth and of nature to knowing their bodies in the biblical sense.

17

The bibliophile's hands were working fast in the pile of old books when he pulled out *Century of Dishonor*. Which he pondered—not his field, not his century—then put back. But his fingertips, clean to the naked eye, kept staining his keyboard as if with red dirt. He returned to buy the book, but it was gone. Out of print, out of sight, so he set his mind to clearing his keys of their building, blushing film. His words stayed black, his fingers white, but the color often returned to the keys, booked by his prints. The dead are powerless?

18

The mythomaniac's back. This time in lab cap and gown, rubber gloves, and mask. He enjoys the irony of this forensic persona. Seeing is believing, reduced to the expert testimony of photographic exhibits. The deed will be scoped from the inside out and its truth known as it is shown. His autopsy will be the jewel in the crime and he needn't say a word to turn himself in. He will simply take the stand and open his belly to the click and whirr of cameras turned on the live icon of the gutsy stench of his surpassing eloquence.

19

There's a killer born every minute. And every minute one earns the name. Then learns to cop a plea. Cain suffered from low self-esteem. And on. And on. And the Big-J can't understand why her room has become a three-ring circus where some die, some roll over, and some fly through the air with the greatest of ease. Patriarchy's mad again. Justitia tries to calm the old man with a kiss on the mouth but gives up when he bites off his own tongue. He does this bit in two shows a day daily, waiting to be booked for a world tour.

20

A family portrait. The memories it jogs diverge, then slip away. Then it will be all that matters. A complete stranger for strangers to study. To find what they can't see of themselves, they spin their gaze into a weave so close nothing, they think, but "dross" will pass through. But they are not so good at this retrieval business and keep losing stuff blink by blink. A record runoff. Still they do try to get the picture, then pause to pose for one of themselves. What stays of them after they scatter stares out and asks, "What's the matter?"

21

Betrayal. Of the mind by the body. Of the person by the mind. No wonder it points everywhere, sweetfully spreading to its offending members. No joint is safe from its vengeful inflammations. Think of it as the vital fire ant, or the bait that bites back. Not much good comes of it, but it keeps on coming. Like compound interest. That you can depend on. So it's always lying around this dump. Our best—shhh, you'll wake it—EF/don't forget AR/EYE/EE/EN/DEE. But then somebody better keep an eye on us. It's constitutional. Warp. Woof.

22

Dogless, the Gestapo agent failed to sniff out Hans Rudelsheim, hidden behind some clothes in his friend Ina's bathroom closet. "And this is the closet," she said as casually as she could and the search of her house ended. A brief satisfaction. Till later that year, '43 March, the mouth of a neighbor's friend opened against him and swallowed him whole (*Hold not thy peace, O God of my praise*), as easy as counting to four: Alive in Leiden—1-2-3-4—in Treblinka smoke. Smelled for miles. But they denied it, though not godless.

23

What will the unborn archaeologist see when she one day holds the puzzle key under the light? She doesn't know it's a key, though she has guessed what it is. An apparition. She is herself inside the puzzle. It is everywhere. But where from? A puzzle. And how to x-ray and record this thing she is amazed she can hold. It seems drawn to her and makes her think of everything she ever wanted. She broods on this translucent egg but cannot hatch it. Undead, it beams instead on her. Without a word or sound. Unlocks itself inside her.

24

The prophet contemplates the Great Escape. It has been done, he's sure. So many names crowd his line of vision. His eyes cross upon two: Buddha and Houdini. The weight. The weight of the earth is killing. Sickman, Oldman, Deadman. The fathom-long longing one. For light. Lightness. Who would have thought so much of it could come in a single night. Out of this cloak of darkness, what a show! What a showman! Headline reads **MAN SHUNS DYING UNTO DEATH**. No sham, he knows. The story follows of making a void into a garden.

25

The mythomaniac knows he is losing touch. Resolves to turn himself into a manometer. An elegant, simple U. There is none so rare or vacuous who may escape the precision of his measure. From now on he'll just point a finger, so to speak, with purely dactylic eloquence at you. Your force, your distress, your commerce—given to the exact degree in his quicksilver discourse. He also knows you think you deserve better and more, but wants you to consider the pressure you put on him to run so true. Why he must be poison to your taste.

26

At times he really believes he's the beautiful dreamer. Which makes him anxious. As does the fear that Justitia will take him by the ear one day. But since he swims his dark waters with the magisterial maneuvers of a shark, his teeth make short denial of his self-doubts. Still, every time he sings *weep no more, my lady* he wonders if it will work. If it does he has praise only for his tongue and throat. Yet the deep sinking within which nothing shines bright, he cannot tear away. When he wakes unto himself he dives back into dream.

27

Naturally, they have each other only. Despite wishes from birth to be chosen. By water. By knife. By secret language. Anger that it is not so divides them, and *vox populi* grows a short fuse. Finally, they only want each other's. And everything else's. And would light the fuse every time to get it but for some dreadful mystery inside that calls them to give account. Well, some. And the surviving animals might be happy about that. That they will wrestle all night for a blessing. Even with the one from the black hole they have made here.

28

If the center has not held it's because it has become self-centrifugal and keeps the appearance of not running away altogether by clinging by its nails to its circumargin long enough to give the prophet a picture of immanent disaster. The archaeologist sees no such thing and keeps circling and diving. Whatever she can clutch radiates, a pressed flower that blooms in her head. Justitia still rides her circuit, knees gripped at a 45° tilt. And the mythomaniac concurs with them all by telling tales from the book of virus.

29

They cannot but make and take pictures of themselves. Yes, they are fruitful and multiply. Have of themselves in good store. And these things they do their utmost to understand and explain: pictures of angels speaking to them, pictures of themselves open-mouthed and rotting in great heaps. And think they're very good at it, better still at conceiving how they get it. Itself a picture of their fecundity. Yet best they are at the makings themselves—out of any material on earth and in their heads. It's just the subject they cannot change.

30

And they have made of themselves such instruments of beauty and terror. The world rings with their sound. All in the name of some kind of love. Whose ways cannot be counted. Or counted on. For it can come out of both sides of a mouth. And still sound fine. Or read out backwards. In stirring red letters. (They could dance on the stars.) But fettered each to each by an iron will, they feel the edge underfoot. Then call with their lovely faces for a greater love to encircle them and sing themselves to peace. Surround, surround.

Mother and Child. Water color and ink on paper. 5" x 7."

Ommatidium. Acrylic on paper. 9" x 12."

L'âge d'or. Water color on paper. 15" x 18."

1892. Water color on paper. 9" x 12."

1892

La partie de croquet

It is from corner to corner
the keen half light of dusk time
and everything the picture holds
it holds in the integrity of this light.
Occupying the front from left to right for two-thirds
of its sixty-three and a half inch width are five figures
—two men, two women, and a dog—
variously engaged in a game of croquet
while in the upper right five young women
a little less than half the height of the women in the front
appear to be dancing or playing a game of tag or blind man's bluff.
At the top left a branch of light green foliage overhangs
the croquet party, paralleled at the bottom
by two large greenish-brown bushes, separated by a strip of grass
which continues beyond the second central bush to fill
the picture's space to its right border and up two-thirds
of its fifty and three-quarter inch height.
The croquet party occupies the space between branch and bushes
against a dark green and brown background
—suggesting thickly growing trees and shrubs—
which in its full extension from edge to edge rises
just beyond the croquet party and flows into the upper right corner
for the remaining one-third of the picture's height
thus forming where it meets the grass a short horizontal line
that bisects the dancing figures approximately at the waist.
Parallel to this line just below the dancing figures a dark green
brown speckled leafy branch reaches into the picture out of its right side.
Directly above the dancers near the right top corner are three
irregular yellow-orange shapes that denote gaps in the heavy foliature
in which the waning light of day's end glows.

ou Crépuscule

Though comprised of five individuals, from left to right: a standing man in front of whom another sits, two women standing with a dog between them (these latter three occupying the center of the canvas), the croquet party's configuration consists primarily of three almost equiponderant, vertical human columns of a common height, roughly equal to a little more than half the picture's. Since its lowest visible limit runs above the picture's bottom at a level about one-fifth its full height, this arrangement then draws the central and major share of the total space. The two men stand and sit near the left edge, both of them looking directly across the picture to the right, which is to say, to their left. The standing man, of somewhat smaller stature, wears a straw hat and an off-white suit, both of which are tinged with green, the suit lightly, the hat more deeply, reflecting the dark background, in whose depth he is placed farther back than any of his companions. He has brown hair, a thin moustache, wears a pale yellow shirt, a short black cravat, and delicately holds in his fingers the handle of his mallet—the top of which reaches the bottom of his necktie—directly in front of himself, right hand just below the left, whose elbow is raised to point in the same direction he looks. He does not appear in full figure, for his lower half is blocked by the seated man, whose legs as well as what he sits upon are, in turn, concealed by the first and larger of the two bushes at the bottom of the picture. Wearing a tan shepherd's cap, a dark brown plaid jacket with large square checks, a white shirt and short dark brown cravat, the seated player holds upright in his left hand his mallet shaft, whose top rises to a level just above his cap at the same height as the standing player's elbow. The seated man's left elbow is also bent to the right, the direction in which he looks. He has a brown beard, tinted with green about the chin. Standing beside him, the first woman bends her neck and shoulders slightly forward and to her left as she concentrates upon setting up a shot on a croquet ball that lies just in front of her between the two bushes. Though her lower right side is partially covered by the extremities of the first shrub, she stands full figure in a long dress that reaches the ground. With a high V-neck and puffed sleeves cuffed at mid-forearm, the dress, which matches the color of the standing man's off-white, green tinted jacket, is adorned with a delicate pattern of small leaves or flowers. She wears a grey sash around her waist and holds her mallet handle with right hand below the left. Poised several inches above the ground, the brown mallet head appears in full side view parallel to the ground as the shaft rises to her waist in a direct line with the V in her dress, her chin, and her line of vision as she looks down at the ball. The inclination of her head and upper body amply displays her reddish tinted brown coiffure subtly against the dark background. With her left hand on the top of the mallet at the level of her sash, her left elbow, like those of the two men, is also bent to the right, its curve's end reaching the exact mid-point of the picture's width. Directly below her elbow, a small white pointer with a brown spot over its left eye and ear and another on its right flank stands between her and the second woman and stares intently at the brown croquet ball. The downward curve of its trim pointing body matches the bend of the woman's elbow, and its tail makes a taut loop at the top of its form. The second woman, whose presentation contrasts least with the dark backdrop, stands with her back to us, head tilted slightly to the left, as she, too, concentrates on the lie of the ball. She wears a full-length long sleeved dress of irregular checks, the largest of which are charcoal grey juxtaposed with smaller checks of green and red. There are three small yellow ribbons in her dark neck-length hair, which is heavily tinted with the deep green of the background, which almost claims her. A black sash hangs loosely from her narrow waist, and her right hand rests on her hip, her right elbow thus bending in congruity with the left elbows of her companions as it curves and closes with the irregular edge of the picture's central dark background as it rises into the upper right corner. The bottom of her dress and feet are obscured by the second bush, to the upper right of which two closely set hoops stand in the grass. Four black stemmed white flowers grow below and to the right of them, while another croquet ball with one white stripe lies to the right of the bush in direct approach to the hoops. The grassy area has been sparsely speckled with white, in broad strokes below the ball the first woman addresses and in dots near the feet of the young women in the distance. In the lower left corner two large light green, delicately touched with red, flowers stand against the bush approximately at the mid-point of its height in the direct line with the seated and standing men.

The five dancing figures in the upper right corner play in a slightly brighter light. Four of them, three to the left and one to the right of a central figure who has her back to us, face her as they move away from her. The two on the far left, the first of whom is already partially concealed behind the dark brown and green brushwork of the central background, are moving in that direction. The third figure of this group moves in the opposite direction, towards the fourth, who moves out of the picture to the right of the central figure, who leans to the left with both arms partially extended. A violet sash criss-crosses her waist and hips, and the bottom of her dress and feet are covered by the leafy branch that reaches into the picture from the right. They all wear full-length white dresses, and their brown hair has been highlighted in orange and red.

In the upper left hand corner in the light green of the overhanging branches in a yellow unrepeated elsewhere in the picture in small printed characters appear the name **Bonnard** and immediately beneath it the year **1892**.

Verticals
from the heart
(as in a poem)
to the eye
by the plumb
of his hand
whose weight
appoints height
the downwards
upon which
is built
outward
to the brim

The front of a picture is its brim. Every picture must be "filled" to its brim in the sense that there will be neither lure nor room in it for anything more than what brings it to that capacity of presentation the painter must know how to recognize as well as to realize.

VERTICALS
The front of a picture is
FROM THE HEART
its brim. Every picture
(AS IN A POEM)
must be "filled" to its brim
TO THE EYE
in the sense that there will
BY THE PLUMB
be neither lure nor room in it
OF HIS HAND
for anything more than what
WHOSE WEIGHT
brings it to that capacity
APPOINTS HEIGHT
of presentation
THE DOWNWARDS
the painter must know
UPON WHICH
how to recognize
IS BUILT
as well as
OUTWARD
to realize.
TO THE BRIM

SESTINA DU CRÉPUSCULE

A little world self-contained, believed Pierre
and painted himself into the picture,
the standing man in straw hat happiness
beneath his name, who holds within his gaze
the scene, recalled by color not invention,
in which he found himself and friends at dusk.

At play in Le Grand-Lemps one day at dusk,
Charles, Berthe, Noisette, Andrée, and Pierre
with a ring of young girls, an invention
through design of a prophetic picture
of what may be born by hand from a gaze
into life's poem, its innermost happiness:

To prolong such joy, beautify happiness
discovered in the lucky group at dusk
in eighteen ninety-two, quickened the gaze
to express itself and subject Pierre
to the laws of the nature of his picture.
So he followed feeling, not invention.

Yet the laws of nature gave invention
to great machines beyond his happiness,
explosions unsighted in his picture,
fiery vapors deferred from the pure dusk
of this time of friends at croquet. Pierre
and they breathe forever the air in his gaze.

Their movement in this moment of his gaze
haunts those who search and sound it to invent
some meaning for the common poise Pierre
feeds upon and serves, the course of happiness
without a hitch. Their pleasure at dusk
exists in the image he has pictured

of it for them—held back in the picture,
the ring of girls that almost slips his gaze
but stays, secure in the last light of dusk.
Serene mystery becomes the invention
of the carefree account of happiness
they figure un-invisibly for Pierre.

So gaze now, viewer, without invention
upon this picture of dusk-time happiness,
your little world self-contained, believe Pierre.

VOLUNTARIES

1

Wellfleet, 10:30 AM 7/6/79, from the deck:

Voluntar-
ily I'll submit
           to the receptions
of the moment.
        My will be done
in whatever reaches me/
               squabbling finches
at the feeder—
         nary a meal in peace
in the strife-filled world of birds
                  and who's to say
it's that much smaller than our own?
Now one eats alone
          its little head bobbing
as it sways on the perch
            —now swoops
another species—lil' chickadee—
               and another till
no one eats now.
        The air fills up
with calls from branches.

2

Wellfleet, 2 PM 7/9/79, from the deck:

Antennae up!
                Bird bath business
very good
           though they also shit in it
and drink there too.
                    My sneeze could drive
them off in a feathery cloud (of many colors,
an involuntary deprivation
                        of their pleasure
but they'd be back
                sure as despised politicians
really do enjoy a sex life
despite efforts at cocktail parties
to punish by withholding it from them.

Sir Blackbird flutters in the fountain
as Lady Cardinal alights in the feeder.

3

Wellfleet, 9:30 AM 7/13/79, from the deck:

Earlier over the first cup of coffee
browsing in *The Norton Anthology of Modern Poetry*
my eye took in Paul's dates as page 1142 flipped by:
    November 24, 1926
    September 13, 1971.
                        He died 2 months and 11 days
short of his 45th birthday
                having made much poetry
many friends
        and his share of mistakes.
                        By whose
will or what plan
        (if any) did it end for him
at that time and in that way?
                  And goes on for me
coincidentally
        2 months and 11 days
from my 45th birthday.
            Our lives—
                  each one alone
                  and all together—
seem to make a pattern
along whose edge we run
putting in our bits and pieces
until, overtaken, we become
permanent parts of it—

      knitted up into the design
those left along its edge keep glimpsing.
            Hail

Clotho   Lachesis   Atropos
           All Hail!
So this Friday the 13th
I write, make plans
and think about the past.
       By the force of what I
will call some kind of grace
when I close my eyes tonight
       I'll still see
the fields of seaweed at Wednesday morning's low tide
and the luminous greens of the freshly watered garden.

4

Wellfleet, 12:30 PM 7/24/79, from the deck:

I have despoiled their dormitories
at the four corners of the house,
little mattresses of grass, mud,
pine needles, packed in the leaders
covering but not plugging the downspouts.
One watched me from the roof
and broadcast a shriek when it
understood what I was up to.
Was this an event well-suited
for a disaster movie for our birdies
just as the destruction of Les Halles
was for the rats of Paris?
They say hundreds of thousands
were displaced—can't you see them
streaming out from under the Place
des Innocents—and took up
residence in the surrounding neighborhoods,
giving up the city's stomach
for the bowels of its restaurants.
Nothing so grand in this our province.
After the realization and reproach
they have returned to work
rebuilding what the Thing on the Ladder
has destroyed, for it also changes
the water daily and fills
two feeders Tuesdays and Saturdays.

5

Wellfleet, 12:15 PM 8/21/79, from the deck:

Pulling away
                for good or before
coming together
                      as in pre-foreplay resistance,
seriously insincere,
                          or the hooked bluefish's final stand
—often a leap for life
                      after it's seen the boat,
a relatively repulsive sight.
                        Pulling away
and coming together
                  two bodies on a bed
on a floor   on a screen/
                      on the deck
the heart of the first eviscerated blue,
last of the catch,
                      separated from the guts and still beating
pumping away
              in and out
                        in purple glory.
He never saw that
before says the mate
                  throwing it overboard.

6

New York, 12:30 AM 10/25/79, from the desk:

Wanting to write a poem for Charles Bukowski
I put a frozen pizza in the oven
start on another sixpack
and wait for inspiration
by staring at the roaches
walking in and out of the pile of laundry on my floor

when the downstairs bell rings
but, expecting nobody, I don't buzz back
probably some asshole forgot their key
—there are assholes everywhere you know
by now the apartment bell rings
and I go see which of my women
it could be and open the door on
a skinny young guy about twenty
who says, "Mr. Bukonomou? I have reason
to believe I am your son." To which I,
"Or maybe just one of those assholes
this world is full of, sonny."

But I ask him in out of the hall
as he starts to explain the detective work
that led him to me as "genetic father"
and I tell him he's too runty
to be a son of mine because my seed
is a stout-hearted seed whether it grows

up to be boys or poems—and Christ
I've seen Tom Clark poems
that are more substantial than he is!

Since he looks like he could use it
I ask him to share the pizza
and have a beer with me and talk
on condition he'll stop this
"you're my daddy" crap—Hell
I've never been anywhere near
Council Bluffs, which is where he says
it all began for him according to his
"real mama" whom he tracked down
in Kansas City two weeks ago
recent polaroid of whom he shows
to which I will only say, "Yeah,
real natural looking mama!"

Then with a squint-smile like a midwife
I open the oven door—
and deftly yank out the rising, bubbling sun.

7

New York, 12:15 AM 11/7/79, from the tub:

Conatus ter
        I've dreamed in Latin
only because I read it somewhere,
                          "Tried thrice"?
Where? When?
              On the third,
                      Virgil
Aeneids two and six:
                      Ter conatus ibi collo dare bracchia circum,
                      ter frustra comprensa manus effugit imago,
                      par levibus ventis volucrique simillima somno.
                    "On the three tries he threw his arms
                    around her neck," Creusa's
                              (beloved wife left for dead
                              in the burnt out city)
                  "around his neck," Anchises'
                              (dear father
                              departed at
                              Drepanum)
                  "three failed embraces as the form fled his hands
                  like a light wind but most like a dream with wings."
Thus only may *conatus*
stand over *frustra*.

8

New York, 3 PM 6/4/80, at the desk:

Calling your book *Eve's Rib*?
As if getting even were possible?
You know as well as I
a good woman is as hard to find
though a woman's a woman for a' that an' a' that
even one of those
                stouthearted women
                              a woman o' war.
Just ask the woman in the street
                      or the one in the moon.

9

New York, 10 AM 6/5/80, at the desk:

When an old black bagman,
finding a discarded half grapefruit
behind the Texaco Station
on Lafayette Street, Brooklyn,
opposite the campus gate,
kneels and crosses himself
and then consumes it,
                       to which department do we refer?
Religion?
       Psychology?
              Modern Dance?
                      Urban Affairs?
We have so many—
        there ought to be a right one.

10

Wellfleet, 10 AM 7/18/80, on the deck:

Here lies June Bug on its back
rigor mortis evident
even in one so light, so empty.
When I flip it over
four pairs of red leggys
hold it up as if poised
to spring. Might as well
be its own memorial.

11

Wellfleet, 2:15 PM 7/26/80, from the deck, for James Lechay:

If I were a painter still
I'd do my new thistle feeder
in a narrow vertical plane
with its wire loop hanging on a branch
angling across the left top corner
its bright orange cap
its tube full of thistle shining black in the sunsray
tiny perch strokes of tan
a swath of pure yellow finch
with a downward pointing to the right line of black
flat of wing against the lambent green light.

12

Wellfleet, 4:30 PM 8/23/80, from the deck:

Personification comes
a lunchtime guest
out of the northeast
that sweeps half my chips
clean out of their dish
off the table and over
deckside/ a blast
as both hands raise
my sandwich to a mouth
that does not bite.

13

Wellfleet, 9:80 AM 7/14/81, from the deck:

Almost a year has passed
since I last made a voluntary
and now I ask myself in one to account for it.
In that close-to-a-year,
I have gone on strike
for 38 days, which cramped
my work and life style
and caused me to worry about money
for the next 7 months
even though we won.
Each of my parents underwent
successful surgery and I have seen them,
I have written book reviews,
finished my Philodemos translations,
written and delivered a paper on Dante,
had interviews for 3 jobs, which crowded
my psyche and fantasy life
and caused me to worry again
about more or less money
and the reasons why I didn't get the jobs,
though I believe in losing them I won.
On the other hand, I had no affairs,
which consume time and money like mad.
So why should my poetic output for this period
amount to one: AMERIKI Book Two Part IV?
I can quote Edward Hopper's

"One good picture is worth a thousand
inferior ones," for a winning explanation.
Or I can say, "I don't know,"
as if it meant I don't take the loss seriously.
Truth is, I cannot explain the hiatus, nor will I
make or grant excuse. I'll volunteer
that though I cannot account for the phenomenon otherwise,
yet possibly it might be otherwise accounted for,
and forget it now that I've resumed.

14

Wellfleet, 10:15 AM 7/23/81, from the deck but at the earlier behest of Kenneth Bernard:

One Soma Golden wrote last winter in the *Times*,
    The famous Hippocratic oath that new physicians still take,
    includes a refusal to give women instruments for abortions.
    But Hippocrates advised women to end unwanted pregnancies
    without instruments, by leaping seven times into the air.
Could he have been serious?
Could he have known of a case or two
in which he believed this had actually occurred?
My first recollection of abortion (without the word)
goes back to my childhood
when I overheard a whispered phrase (in Greek),
"She took a bath,"
and it occurred to me that that bath
had something to do with babies,
though somewhat later did I connect
the baby with the bathwater.
Did a young woman of Cos who had miscarried
come to Hippocrates to say everything had been fine
until she went down to the sea one recent day,
and after her swim could not resist
her old habit of dancing naked in the sunlight,
leaping into the air 5, 6, 7 times,
and the doctor did connect her loss with those saltations,
finding advice, thereby, for unwanting mothers?
Was that self-prescribed bath forty years ago

simply part of the Hippocratic legacy,
if the doctor will not do it, it isn't wrong to try yourself?
Or, to bring the question up to its latest terms,
to argue, as does Soma, that politicians
leave it to women to decide for their own bodies?
I was suddenly reminded of Soma Golden
by a party of mother/daughter nudies
at Bound Brook Island yesterday.
When one of the women got up to swim,
I could see none of the customary lines
that contrast buttocks and breasts with the rest.
She emerged from the water about 100 yards away,
leaped 1, 2, 3, 4 times into the air,
then cracked her hair like a whip in the sun.

15

Wellfleet, 10:30 AM 7/30/81, from the deck but also at the earlier behest of Kenneth Bernard, who had sent on a card, *The dream is an involuntary act of poetry*—Jean Paul Richter:

So it is and provides a source as well
for those voluntary acts we call poems
because we try to make their elements at every level rhyme.
The dream, too, may rhyme in its sights and sounds or structure
for its dreamer—but only for a listener and differently
after it's been pumped into the other act of poetry,
even at the level of the simplest telling:
I saw a tall, solitary figure of a man
walking down a darkened New York street.
Because he was dressed all in black, I couldn't see his face
without rushing up to him and as I did
I recognized Abraham Lincoln and exclaimed,
"Mr. President, you mustn't walk these streets alone at night!"
Between this as involuntary act of poetry
and its articulation as example here,
lie varieties of resonance and correspondence
whose flow I cannot nor would control.
I would merely draw from it the dream direct
or in other forms for the lines that give my poem
its life and power to relieve and relive.
When we dream, we stand within rather than apart
from the poetic act, capable of an enstatic experience,
which—like ancient acts of poetry—
may be translated but never duplicated;

but when we pipe and fix our voluntary rhymes,
we have the chance for an ecstatic one,
to know that though of us they have their independence,
to have the chance to offer them like drinks of water from our house.

16

Wellfleet, 4:45 PM 8/5/81, from the deck:

My personal award
for barber of the year—
to the cottontail higgeldy
hop that gave a perfect
crew cut to a whole row
of late planted lettuce.

17

Wellfleet, 1 PM 9/4/81, from the deck:

As the time approaches to say good-bye again,
I have filled your two feeders,
Chickadees, Goldfinches, Purplefinches,
Mourning Doves, Bluejays, shy Cardinal,
Grackles galore and Nuthatches,
and as I watch you feed, feeding myself
on a piece of cheddar and potato chips,
remember an afternoon earlier this summer
when I was driving out of the dump
suddenly aware of a great formation
of gulls flying directly overhead
exactly in the same direction as I
that was right in the middle of their squadron
for a few seconds moving along
in perfect synchrony.
The sensation born of that accident
will always stay as a felt flash
of the art of nature—a peek at the primal sketch
under the huge design that holds the details
of our separate seeming journeys
down to our apparent parting on Tuesday.

PLAY/FABLES

PLAY/FABLE 1

...blown from a branch
                to the deck rail
an Inchworm gets the part—
being omnivorous and lacking
a middle pair of legs—
                of Everyman
and immediately begins to work
crawling back and forth along the stage
looping his shiny green way beautifully:
                Humps his middle
                    pulls his rear towards his front
                              which he pushes forward
then begins again
                humps his middle
                    pulls his rear towards his front
                              which he pushes forward
then begins again
                humps his middle
                        all in a fluid motion
back and forth across the long rail-world
back and forth in a bit of a rut
checking out the edge from time to time
                        for an alternative
(a breeze gracious as the one that brought him
could carry him away)
                    back and forth
back and forth—really into his role now
when Death
                      brilliantly portrayed by a Bluejay
                              enters...

PLAY/FABLE 2

A fishing boat captain out of Cape Cod
Turned a young woman into a frog.
It wasn't magic, it wasn't voodoo,
Just his rod, for it comforted as few do.

After high school and a couple of office jobs, she began to hang out at the dock, a fisherman's groupie, and determined he should have her. So, though she could have been his daughter, he took her on as wharf-wife. She drove him faithfully to and from town and helped him undress at night. Gradually, she was forced to share his kisses more and more with the glasses and bottles. He could cruise the floor of a party, his handsome blond head bobbing up at the coffee-table's edge, and down all of the drinks on it in their "delusious," caustic variety. She became desperately hungry and began to blow-up. By the time he was almost impervious to sobriety, her transformation was complete, and he had her taken away.

PLAY/FABLE 3

A man cultivated a garden
of lost opportunities
planting their seeds in neat rows:
one for the jobs he'd wanted but never got
another for the investments and sure-thing bets he never made
there was a row for friendships he'd failed to accept
another for the chances he hadn't taken to even old scores
a row for the women he never fucked with
another for those he believed he hadn't fucked with enough
and a large plot for the unfulfilled plans he was sure he could have
    realized.
Mostly, once planted, they grew and flourished
for his soul was well-disposed to contain and nourish them
as the indispensable flowerings of what was never-to-be
which he could then keep to contemplate in all seasons.
But a few he treated with very special care
the potent secret centerpieces of "the other life"
whose leaves from time to time he would trim
and toss into a salad whose days he could almost taste
but for the vinegar and gall it was dressed in.

*NASHVILLANELLE
& OTHER RIMES*

NASHVILLANELLE

My left brain says you've split this time for real,
The pick-up's gone, the mobile home's no more,
My right brain cries this ache will never heal.

It's true, I two-timed you, acted like a heel,
Kept sowin' wild oats just like I'd done before;
My left brain says you've split this time for real.

Your hair-do grew with every hurt I'd deal;
Your wounded pride now cuts me to the core.
My right brain cries this ache will never heal.

It's too late now, and you can't see me kneel
to beg you back; though askin' from the floor,
My left brain says you've split this time for real.

I'll walk, walk on, with nothin' to conceal;
You're gone, I'm beat, you've evened up the score.
My right brain cries this ache will never heal.

So keep on truckin' darlin', and don't feel
Bad for me—I'll live—but never to ignore
My left brain says you've split this time for real,
My right brain cries this ache will never heal.

LOVE'S LETTER
 ψ

To have taken off our clothes
to take the sleep
that would have been
Oh so sweet then—
awake
       my long hard body
against your soft long body
to make
a vibrant psi of them.

KYRIELLE
A song for September

I run like a youth down the street—
I think, as leaves surround my feet
in a brown swirl of days, off who?
off me, green leaves are precious few.

I sing like a kid in a choir,
off key, then strum destiny's lyre
to make it true, O make it true
for me, one precious song with you.

I dream like a boy every day
of you, it takes my breath away:
the tree and we come into view—
these precious days I'll spend with you.

LAMENT OF THE MAFIOSO MAKER

I who wrote whole from urban hate,
Abjuring Nature in ev'ry state,
Now commit all to parody.
    Timor Hitman conturbat me.

Slave to Fortune, that old puttan',
I turn my learning to put on,
And join in her fraternity.
    Timor Hitman conturbat me.

All that's written's grist for my mill,
Point ev'ry line at Sendupville,
Demand for my stuff equality.
    Timor Hitman conturbat me.

Black hand can squeeze another's phrase,
Black Hand can graft on t 'others' praise,
yet clutch its own paternity.
    Timor Hitman conturbat me.

I learned to do the catalogue,
Mock-encomium cum epilogue,
The elephantine elegy.
    Timor Hitman conturbat me.

Though Nature's works I vilify,
Her apes I ape with college try,
However scornful of degree.
    Timor Hitman conturbat me.

Like younger me, he's packin' iron,
Blow'n 'em away with critical firin'.
Must I accept this irony?
> *Timor Hitman conturbat me.*

I pray I'm safe in academe,
Self-reified, so it would seem,
In Pastoral proleptically.
> *Timor Hitman conturbat me.*

IL GRAN VEGLIO DI CRETA

> "Dentro dal monte sta dritto un gran veglio,"
> *Inferno* XIV. 103

He is the dream we choose not to remember,
buried where once the green life quilted our land
of golden tales of the cradled years before
it was wasted, the center of the center.
He's hidden now under the softly padded
tracks of foxes and wolves, beneath the hairline
of a king who cannot let go what he knows
has gone out of his mind but not his center.
A guide calls or is called, with lips that are blessed
with power to unearth the lost dream of him
whose tears feed the rivers of our barren hopes,
and says of him to us he is the center
of our story and our brains and that he falls.

TRANSLATIONS

HEDYLOS
from *The Greek Anthology,* #199

Wine and wily Cheers and Nick's
sweet lovin' put Aggie straight to sleep;
her maidenly passion's spoils lie still be-
fore Love's Goddess, all of them wet with her scent,
her sandals and the soft top that fits round her titties,
sole witnesses to how she slept as he tore off a piece.

THE GIRL NEXT DOOR

I wanted to teach you a little song,
In Greek, so these Latins won't understand:
Between your breasts a star is hung,
A bagful of parsley's in your hand.
Girl born beautiful, you've nothing wrong.
Perfectly shaped as a silver band.
Wherever you set your graceful feet
You scent the neighborhood and our street.

Itela na su masu 'na sonetto,
Grico, na mi to fsèrune i Latini:
An astèri vastà mesa's to petto,
Vastà mia chiantan afse petrosini:
Oriamu jènomeni, en ehi deffeto.
Ce lavurata ise sa t'asimi:
'Ci pu pratù ta pòjasu garbata
Mirìzi i jetonìa ce oli i strata.

CXXXIII. *Studi dialetti Greci della terra d'Otranto.* Edited by Giuseppe Morosi. Lecce, 1870.

C.P. CAVAFY

HALF AN HOUR
(1917)

Never made it with you and don't expect
I will. Some talk, a slight move closer,
as in the bar yesterday, nothing more.
A pity, I won't deny. But we artists
sometimes by pushing our minds
can—but only for a moment—create
a pleasure that seems almost physical.
That's why in the bar yesterday—with the help
of alcohol's high power—I had
a half hour that was completely erotic.
I think you knew it and
stayed on purpose a little longer.
That was really necessary. Because
with all my imagination and the spell of the drinks,
I just had to see your lips
had to have your body near.

IN THE MONTH OF ATHYR
(1917)

With difficulty I read   what's on this ancient stone.
"L[OR]D JESUS CHRIST."   I recognize a "SO[U]L."
"IN THE MON[TH] OF ATHYR"   "LEFKIO[S] FELL ASLEEP."
At the mention of years,   "HE LI[VE]D TO THE AGE OF,"
the Kappa Zeta reveals   he was young when he fell asleep.
On a worn away part I can see   "HI[M] ... ALEXANDRIAN."
There follow three lines   that are extremely mutilated,
but I can make out a few words—   like "OUR T[EA]RS," "GRIEF,"
then "TEARS" again,   and "MOURNED B[Y] HIS [F]RIENDS."
It seems to me Lefkios'   love was great and deep.
In the month of Athyr   Lefkios fell asleep.

Athyr: Egyptian goddess of love and the dead, whose month corresponds to October-November.   **Kappa Zeta** = 27.

THE CITY
   (1910)

You said, "I'll go to another shore, I'll go to another land.
Another city will turn up better than this.
Everything I do is doomed to miss,
and my heart—like a dead man—lies in a grave.
How long can my mind wither in this place?
Whatever I see, wherever my eye falls,
it's this black wreck of a life that calls,
here where I've spent these years, wasted and ruined."

You won't find another shore, you won't find a new land.
This city will trail you. You'll walk the same
old streets. In the same old neighborhoods you'll age,
and in the same old houses you'll turn gray.
You'll aways end up in this city. As for elsewhere—don't stay
hopeful—there's no ship for you, nor road to take.
Just as in this tiny corner you've made
a mess of your life, in all the world it stands in ruin.

ACCORDING TO THE RECIPES OF ANCIENT GRECO-SYRIAN MAGICIANS
(1931)

"What distillate of magic herbs
can I find," said an aesthete,
"what distillate according to the recipes
of ancient Greco-Syrian magicians
that will for a day (if its power
won't last longer) or for just a moment
take me back to twenty-three,
my friend of twenty-two bring me,
bring him back—with his beauty and his love?

"What distillate can I find according to the recipes
of ancient Greco-Syrian magicians
that will, as part of this trip back,
restore as well our little room?"

GEORGE SEFERIS

LES ANGES SONT BLANCS
for Henry Miller

Tout à coup Louis cessa de frotter ses jambes l'une contre l'autre et dit d'une voix lente: "Les anges sont blancs."—BALZAC, *LOUIS LAMBERT*

Like a sailor in the ship's rigging he slid over the tropic of Cancer
 and the tropic of Capricorn
and it was quite natural he could not stop before us at a human
 height
but looked at us all from the height of a glow-worm or from the
 height of a pine
deeply drawing his breath in the stars' dew or in the earth's dust.
Naked women with bronze leaves from fig trees of Araby
 surrounded him
extinguished street lamps airing the soiled bandages of the great
 city
unshapely bodies birthing centaurs and amazons
as their hair touched the Milky Way.

And days have passed since the moment he first greeted us taking
 off his head and setting it on the iron table
while Poland's shape transformed like ink drunk up by blotting
 paper
and we traveled among island shores bare like strange fish bones
 in the sand
and the whole empty pure white sky was a great pigeon's wing

  with a rhythm of silence
and the dolphins under the colored water darkened quickly like
  the soul's movements
identical with the imagination's movements and with the hands of
  men who grope and kill each other in their sleep
in the great unmarked rind of sleep that wraps us all, common to
  us all, our common grave
with glittering tiny crystals crushed by the motion of reptiles.
And yet everything was white because the great sleep is white and
  the great death
calm serene separated in an endless silence.
And the guinea hen's cackling at dawn and the cock that crowed
  as he fell into a deep well
and the fire on the mountainside raising hands of sulphur and
  autumn leaves
and the ship with forked shoulderblades more tender than the
  first time we lay together in love,
these were things isolated even more than the poem
that you left behind when you fell heavily with its last word
without knowing anything more among the white eyeballs of the
  blind and the sheets
that you unfolded feverishly to cover the procession
of people who won't bleed no matter how often they attack
  themselves with hatchets and fingernails;
these were things apart put elsewhere and the steps of whitewash
descended to the threshold of the past and found silence and the
  door wouldn't open
and you said your friends were knocking loudly with great despair
  and you were with them
but you heard nothing and all around you dolphins rose mutely in
  the seaweed.

And again you fixed your gaze and that man with the bitemarks
    of the tropics in his skin
lowering his dark visor as if he intended to work with a blow-torch
    spoke humbly taking care and pausing at every word:
"The angels are white flaming white and the eye that would confront
    them withers
and there is no other way you've got to become like stone if you seek
    their communion
and when you seek out the miracle you must scatter your blood to
    the eight points of the winds
because the miracle is nowhere if not circulating in the veins of man."

Hydra-Athens, Nov. '38

THE CATS OF ST. NICHOLAS

But still my soul deep within me,
self-taught, sings the Fury's
lyreless dirge and fails
to hold its confidence of hope.
            Aeschylus, *Agamemnon*, 990 f.

"There's the Cat's Cape...," said the captain to me
pointing at a low stretch of shore in the mist,
a deserted beach on Christmas day,
"... and out there to the West, the swell gave birth to Aphrodite;
they call the place Greek's Rock.
Left by ten!"
She had Salome's eyes, the cat I lost last year
and Ramazan, how he'd stare death right in the eye,
days on end in the snow of the East
under a frozen sun
right in the eye days on end, that little hearth god.
Keep moving, traveler.
"Left by ten," murmured the steersman.

... maybe my friend had held back,
between ships now
closed up in a small house with icons
looking for windows behind the frames.
The ship's bell struck

like a coin from a lost city
that falling recalls
alms from another time.

"Strange," the captain continued.
"That bell—given this day—
reminded me of another, one in a monastery.
A monk told me the story
a half-crazy man, a dreamer.

"In the time of the great drought,
—forty years without rain—
the whole island fell to ruin;
the people died and snakes were born.
Millions of snakes on this cape,
thick as human legs
and full of poison.
Those days the monastery of St. Nicholas
belonged to the monks of St. Basil
and they couldn't work the fields
and couldn't put their flocks to pasture;
the cats they raised saved them.
At dawn every day a bell would strike
and they'd troop out in a throng to battle.
All day they'd fight till the hour
the bell rang for their evening feeding.
After dinner the bell struck again
and they'd go out into the night battle.
It was a marvel to see them, they say,
some lame, some blinded, others
missing a nose, an ear, their coats in shreds.

So to the ring of four bells a day
months passed, years, season after season.
Wild, unyielding, and ever wounded
they wiped out the snakes but in the end
they were lost; they could not withstand that much poison.
Like a sunken ship
they left no trace on the foam
not a meow, not a bell.
Hold steady!
                What could the poor things do
day and night struggling and drinking
the poisonous reptilian blood.
Centuries of poison, generations of poison."
"Hold steady!" heedlessly echoed the steersman.

                                      Wednesday, 5 February 1969

JOSÉ PASCUAL BUXÓ

ETRUSCAN MUSEUM

1
(Woman's Head)

Right now,
installed
among faces that were hers maybe
or that loved her only
as they love her now,
she still looks for a distant mirror
and her lips swell with delight,
her round chin
where the stone sings
with her grace.

Or maybe
here only,
among dark faces
that did not see hers,
is she loved.

2
(Couple)

Reunited in death
by death
who finally holds them both.

Upright,
correct,
with a simple mask of pride
with just a little
uneasy arrogance.

Now made out of wax
and out of clay
an example of dignity fortified.

With the man's arms
giving shelter
in fictitious sweetness
to the wife's shoulders
distant still.

3
(Amphitheater)

There were voices here,
the tumult
of a strange energy;
there were words here
in the incendiary air
and they were heeded.

The heart drowned
in these stones,
then—as they are now—alone,
and joy erupted
like a jet of pus
and maybe someone met his death
among bodies driven
by those
cadenced
words.

4
(Etruscan tomb)

Upon arrival,
some traces scarcely
on the wall
where water seeps.

And there, in the shadow
and humidity,
the black stones.

A few remote
marks
and the naked density of the stone,
the silent
miracle
of water.

We squeeze time.
Tomb of time
where these words
too are
superfluous.

Translated with Luis Cortest.

REMEMBERING AN UNSHARED NARRATIVE

Afflicted with a Tithonian dwindling that lasted five years, my father died of "old age" at ninety-six. The agility of his light, quick step, which had always seemed the gift of a lifetime, began to abandon him, at first gradually around the middle of his ninety-first year after he had climbed the roof of his home for the last time to replace a few worn and warped shingles, and then with an alarming acceleration as other signs of physical diminution began to appear, one after the other. That this reduction was happening, as it had to, I understood in some vague way from afar, and my one or two visits a year deposited in my memory a succession of framed appearances in which he moved abruptly through discrete stages of decline and decrepitude. Sitting quietly at the head of the table at family dinners, taking no pleasure in the food before him. Thanking me with the merest of nods after I had shaved him with his electric razor. Leaning lightly into the motion of whoever was available to lead him to the bathroom or bedroom—a weak, unsteady charge, whose wardrobe consisted almost completely of pajamas and bathrobes. It wasn't until this sequence of scenes progressed from one of bedridden frailty at home to one of sunken-cheeked sleep in a hospital room, that I even began to admit the possibility that before long the next, and last, two scenes would be played in a nursing home and the Highwood Cemetery at the foot of Montana's Little Belt Mountains. Yet as long as Clotho kept spinning out the thread of his lifeline, no matter how tenuously, there was easy comfort not to think of Atropos, shears in hand, waiting in the wings to make her entrance.

After that line, spun out of the mountains of northern Peloponnesus all the way to the Rockies of the American northwest, was finally cut, one of these scenes began to assume a crucial importance in my private, unshared narrative of a son's life with his father. It occurred six months before he died, on the first day of my last visit with him in the middle of March, often a season in Montana that feels winter's grip relenting without the slightest sign of spring showing its hand, a time of chilly, apprehensive liminality. It was in his hospital room, to which I had come straight from the airport with the same cousin who had picked me up this and so many times before. He was asleep when we arrived, but he awoke just a few minutes after my cousin and I had sat down on either side of his bed to continue the latest installment of our habitual conversation about what was new in Great Falls. When he opened his eyes he was facing me, and I looked for a sign of acknowledgement of my surprise visit, though I knew he had been told I was coming. Before I could greet him and rise to lean over to kiss him, I was stopped by his expression of curious puzzlement, which lingered in his eyes for a moment before he turned to my cousin and asked him in Greek, "Who is this, Gus?" Chortling, Gus answered roundly, "It's George, Jim." Repeating my name once, almost incredulously, my father turned towards me with a look I will never forget, a look that began as one of agitated self-reproach and ended as one of troubled yet tender recognition. "I'm sorry I did not know you, son." Then he looked away at some point up in the ceiling.

Rising to kiss him, I said something casually dismissive like, "Oh, Papa, that can happen to anyone. It's nothing." But his lingering pensive look and my own fleeting sensation that I had been marked for some kind of unexpected enlightenment argued, for a few more moments, against its insignificance. But these intial reactions gradually wore off, and neither of us mentioned it again. I did not refer to it as my cousin drove me to my parents' home, and I said nothing about it to my mother after we arrived. I am not certain, but I would like to think, that my father no longer remembered his "lapse" when I visited him again that evening, and though I never really forgot it I succeeded in setting it aside for the next few months. Then his death restored it to a definitive standing in my memories of our relationship, and I would never again think of it as a lapse. Accidental or not, whatever its provenance, it was the gift of a condition, a faint yet permanent nimbus that only I knew circled my head.

Becoming fatherless could be reckoned with, but becoming so with an abiding doubt about the solidity of our connectedness was something else. It beckoned me into a state of uncertainty that, despite its unsettling property, maintained a claim of normality. That moment of unrecognition in my father's room in the Montana Deaconess Hospital had become for me a recognition of lasting consequence. That he did not know me as he awoke that March afternoon, no matter how easily or rationally it could be explained away, introduced grounds for questioning all of my self-assured assumptions about how well I had known him. The import of this event rather than the event itself had seized my thoughts, and my memory, which was now all that joined us, ceased to function as an end in itself and opened onto avenues with familiar surroundings that aimed ultimately at unknown destinations. My special images of us together were no longer secure, now that I realized it was only blind faith in my own feelings about them that led me to believe I knew anything concerning his feelings about them. So it came as a surprise that my recollections of him should now shake rather than confirm the confidence of my belief that I had known him well in life. With no one but myself to whom to make the necessary admission, "I'm sorry I did not know you, father," the memories, instead of behaving like simple acts of preservation, sustained the truth that I had indeed not known him as well as I thought I had and that I would spend the rest of my life trying to know him *in memoriam* under the same conditions as I had when he was alive, only now with all illusions eluded.

X-RAY FINISH

LIST OF TITLES FOR STORIES NEVER TO BE WRITTEN IN THE SHORT STORY WRITER'S NOTEBOOK

MY ARCADIA

PAUL'S RIGHTHAND MAN

UNDER THE OTTOMAN

HOW TO PLANT A LAUREL TREE

MIRACLE IN THE VINEYARDS

THE SADDLEMAKER'S SON

OK IN ELLIS ISLAND

BOAT TRAIN TO MONTANA

LUGANO HONEYMOON

ONE NIGHT IN JANUARY

THE PRINCESS OF MATERNITY

VENUS IN LIBRA RISING

STOPWATCH&LISTEN

NEATEST KID IN THE NEIGHBORHOOD

BAKLAVA FOR BREAKFAST

HOW TO STEAL A TEXAS LEAGUER

SICK OF THE GARDEN OF GETHSEMANE

DUCKING THE BISHOP'S KISSER

A BIG STEAL UNDER THE BIG SKY

IMPRESSIONS OF A BARNYARD

THE WINE-DARK LIPS OF NANCY BEATTY

BIG CITY COCOON

SICILIAN REDHEAD

READIN' WRITIN' SMOKIN' & DRINKIN'

LESSONS FROM SOPHIE TUCKER'S LOVER

I WRESTLED THE QUEEN OF LESBOS TO A DRAW

MIDSUMMER NIGHT'S DREAM OF UPSTATE NY

GEM, OR WHATEVER, OF THE OCEAN

A VERY PERSONAL BOHEMIA

SURE, AGAMEMNON'S TOMB

SPOONFUL OF ROSE PETAL PRESERVES

GYPSY CURSE NO JOKE

HEAR THAT ASS, PELOPONNESIAN

BOUZOUKI BLUES

HIGH FEVER, LOW TIDE

ARRIVEDERCI ROMA AGAIN

AGORAPHAGIA

SOCIOPOETICS

WOULD-BE-GOD-DAUGHTER, GOOD-BYE

FROM A GARDEN APARTMENT

THE ENGAGEMENT RING FAIRY

GOING FOR THE NIGHTLIFE

THANK MARGARET SANGER

BLIND DATE IN ISTANBUL

...THAN TO BE IN CAROLINA

AARON, THE SOCIAL REALIST

DIVORCED, DEFROCKED, DETERMINED

COMING TOGETHER

THE ANNIVERSARY ROCK

THE TRIBAL HAIRSTYLIST

ALSO OLGA IN OSLO

AT THIRTY-FIVE YOU'RE ONLY FOURTEEN

I COULDA'BEEN ONE OF THE GREAT ONES

TOBY OR NOT TOBY

A NEW YORK COP IS ONLY HUMAN

ENGLISH 501: REMEDIAL CHAUCER

A GIRLFRIEND'S CAT ALWAYS HATES YOU

THE BASIL KING OF WELLFLEET

MEET MONSIEUR MANET

POEMS IN PICKET LINES

MAKING THE LAND RUN IN A '71 CUTLASS

AN EVENING IN KINGFISHER

ITALY IS NOT A CHRISTIAN NATION

WAIST LINE OF PORK

MEET ME IN THE MALVERN HILLS

PIERRE BONNARD TO THE RESCUE

THE LAW OF LONGEVITY

A DANCING GIACOMETTI

"WHEN I WAS ALIVE…I'M STILL ALIVE?"

IN THE WINNER'S CIRCLE

Aggie's Cheer
Balkan War
Cathy's Boy
Daddy-O
Easy Does It
Fa Sol La
Georgiegeorgy
Howard's Nose
Illinois Line
Johnnina
Kissin' Cousin
LaLoba
Mudcapper's Day
No-No-Nonsense
Osso Bucko
Pascal's Choice
Queenie Mine
RePete
Steamin' Stanley
Toby's Turn
Urdu Stud
Vicarious
Wowwow
X-Ray Finish
Yucatan Ann
Ziegfeld's Filly

AN EVENING IN KINGFISHER

"ENTERING KINGFISHER, OKLAHOMA"
the road sign reads
"THE BUCKLE ON THE WHEAT BELT."
We drive to the Elks Club
where we join three hundred men
with big buckles on their belts
to boost the Sooners & our university
in what is traditionally OSU Aggie territory
drinking & mixing with them, eating "fries"
also known as prairie or mountain oysters
scooped up barehanded
as you hold your beer or bourbon in the other
followed by steaks, ranch style baked beans
homemade cracked wheat bread & more beer
salad fixings with no dressing whatever
strong coffee & no fooling around with dessert.
After the obligatory welcome speeches
the winningest active coach in college football
runs the play he will call this spring
a hundred times throughout the state
and then fields questions:
—"Barry (pronounced Berra), how's the Texas
   game gone turn out this year?"
—"One thing I kin tell you 'bout the Texas
   game fer sure—it's gone be one tough sumabitch!"
—"Barry, could yuh use a sixty-six year old guard?"
—"Give that man another drink."
Somebody does as coach Switzer
closes this appearance with a herpes joke

and a hopeful, if not overconfident
prediction about the coming season.
The macho party & male ritual complete
(exept for those with expectations
based on their consumption of fries)
we move for the doors or bartenders
and I am almost out into the night air
when the sixty-six year old guard pulls
out of the line at the bar & squints
at my crimson-bordered OU name tag
offering his hand to mine which he begins to squeeze
and asks me where I'm from.
—"The university."
—"Well, I kin see that. I mean with a name
 like that where are yuh *from?*
Looking back at his tag
which reads " 'Huck' Rice"
and understanding what he's getting at,
—"Just moved here from New York,
 but I was born in Montana."
He squeezes harder,
—"But that's not an American name."
—"Sure it is, from Greece. (And making a good guess)
 When did your people come over here from Germany, Huck?"
Easing up on the squeeze,
—"Oh hell, we bin here forever."
—"You mean you're native American?"
—"No, no indian. What d'yuh do at OU?"
—"I teach English."
—"With a name like that, yuh teach English?"
—"I run the whole show in English, Huck.
 "I'm chairman of the department, brought in

from New York."
The handshake ends in a tie
and I'm grateful for the summers
spent opening oysters in Wellfleet.
—"Well, George, how d'yuh like workin'
 here among all these Americans?"
—"I told you, Huck, I was *born* here."
—"I like yuh, George, I'd like to talk
 to yuh 'bout your beliefs."
Remembering Roy Rogers' characterization
of Reagan when he was nominated in 1980,
—"Why, I'm 'a fine Christian gentleman,'
 just like you. Only my kind is the oldest,
 Huck. Greek, you know, right back to the
 language of the New Testament (making another
 good guess) while you Lutherans are pretty recent."
Shaking his head,
—"Greek, and yuh teach English
 and don't even have an accent."
—"No, no accent, Huck, perfect English.
   You've got the accent. But give me a
   chance and I'll be back here next year
 sounding just like you."
—"I'd like that, I like yuh, George."
—"So long, Huck, see you next year."
Leaving Kingfisher, I try not to hear
the obvious literary echoes
and focus rather on the odd sincerity
of my dialogue with Huck,
and definitely name him
to my first team offensive line.

BELL-HAIKU

The light on the lake
plays solo on the mist-horn
—no need for the sun.

        Though without halo
        Economou on Como—
        feels *come un angelo.*

                Who's to see the boat?
           Who will count the moonlight's march?
                  Will I miss sunset?

He thinks he hears it
booming over his shoulder
—strike that crossed his eyes.

        The water wears its
             stillness close as the mountains
                  wear the clouds like shawls.

Black and white cut-outs—
mountains and moon enter as
puppets of the night.

Too dimensional—
the lake, mountains, and the town.
Mist-ure screens their depths.

> *Haiku doppio*
> Lake Como in red—
> a dancing Giacometti
> on a black t-shirt:
> in its absent crotch
> imagine Bellagio—
> where better to be?

> Why leave the Villa?
> To recall its splendid days,
> driving to the store.

> As tourists snap me,
> I become their souvenir:
> La Veduta man!

April 28-May, 1993
Villa Serbelloni, Bellagio

BIOGRAPHICAL NOTE

George Economou was born in Great Falls, Montana, on September 24, 1934. He has published six books of poetry and several books on medieval literature. He has also published translations from ancient and modern Greek as well as from a number of medieval languages, most recently William Langland's *Piers Plowman* (University of Pennsylvania Press). His poems, translations, and criticism have appeared in many leading literary and scholarly journals. He has held fellowships for his writing from the New York Council for the Arts, the National Endowment for the Arts, and the Rockefeller Foundation. He earned his A.B. from Colgate University and his M.A. and Ph. D. from Columbia University. He is currently Professor of English at the University of Oklahoma and lives with his wife, poet-playwright Rochelle Owens, in Norman, Oklahoma and Wellfleet, Massachusetts.